Sumo Unlocked
Mastering the Art of the Sumo Deadlift

Ethan R. Reynolds

CONTENTS

INTRODUCTION

Welcome to "Sumo Unlocked: Mastering the Art of the Sumo Deadlift." Within the pages of this comprehensive guide, we embark on a journey that explores the intricacies of one of the most powerful and revered lifts in the realm of strength training - the Sumo Deadlift. Whether you are a novice lifter seeking to perfect your technique or an experienced athlete looking to explore advanced variations, this book aims to equip you with the knowledge and tools necessary to excel in the art of the Sumo Deadlift.

Chapter by chapter, we will delve into every facet of the Sumo Deadlift, uncovering its foundational techniques, advanced variations, and the nuances that make it a challenging yet rewarding movement. We will explore the Sumo Deadlift's distinct setup, foot positioning, and grip variations that form the pillars of a solid foundation. Building upon this, we will investigate how to optimize your stance, hip, and shoulder positioning to ensure optimal performance and safety.

As we progress through this journey, we will venture into the realm of advanced techniques and variations, discovering the Romanian Sumo Deadlift, the Sumo Deadlift High Pull, and the dynamic resistance brought about by incorporating chains or bands. These variations will challenge your explosive power, muscle engagement, and control, elevating your Sumo Deadlift to new levels of strength and prowess.

The path to mastering the Sumo Deadlift does not end with technique and variations alone; it extends to perfecting your form and understanding how to execute the lift with precision and efficiency. We will delve into the role of the back and core engagement, the significance of the knees and shins, and how breathing techniques can enhance your performance and protect against injury.

While the Sumo Deadlift is an undeniably powerful lift, it is crucial to understand the principles of training strategies that drive continual progress and strength gains. Embracing the concept of progressive overload and knowing when to listen to your body for optimal auto-regulation are essential components in your journey of mastering the Sumo Deadlift.

Throughout this book, we emphasize the significance of rest and recovery as vital components of training. Understanding how to integrate rest days and active recovery techniques into your routine will enable you to stay resilient, prevent burnout, and foster long-term progress.

In the pages that follow, we invite you to explore the depths of the Sumo Deadlift, unlock its secrets, and embrace the art of this exceptional lift. Whether you are a seasoned lifter or just beginning your strength journey, this book is designed to offer valuable insights, practical guidance, and inspiration to propel you towards greatness in the Sumo Deadlift.

May this guide be a beacon of knowledge and motivation as you pursue excellence in this remarkable lift. As we embark on this journey together, let us harness the power, finesse, and discipline required to master the art of the Sumo Deadlift and unveil the strength within. Now, let us begin this transformative voyage into the world of "Sumo Unlocked: Mastering the Art of the Sumo Deadlift."

CHAPTER 1:
UNDERSTANDING THE
SUMO DEADLIFT

The Sumo Deadlift, a variant of the conventional deadlift, has become an increasingly popular and effective technique among strength athletes, powerlifters, and fitness enthusiasts alike. Characterized by its wide stance and hand placement within the knees, the Sumo Deadlift offers a unique approach to lifting heavy loads off the ground.

The Sumo Deadlift: An Introduction

At its core, the Sumo Deadlift is a compound movement that targets multiple muscle groups, making it a highly efficient exercise for building strength and increasing overall power. Unlike the conventional deadlift, where the feet are placed shoulder-width apart and the hands grip the barbell outside the knees, the Sumo Deadlift requires a wider stance with the hands positioned inside the knees. This unique configuration alters the mechanics of the lift, emphasizing different muscle groups and placing varied demands on the lifter's body.

In its earliest origins, the Sumo Deadlift found prominence in the sport of sumo wrestling, from which it draws its name. Sumo wrestlers would engage in various strength training exercises to enhance their performance in the ring, and the Sumo Deadlift emerged as a pivotal exercise to develop lower body strength and explosive power. Over time, strength athletes recognized the value of this lift beyond the realm of sumo wrestling, incorporating it into their own training regimens with remarkable results.

Advantages of the Sumo Deadlift

The Sumo Deadlift offers several advantages over the conventional deadlift, making it a preferred technique for certain lifters. One of the key benefits lies in the reduced strain on the lower back. The wide stance allows for a more upright torso position during the lift, leading to a decreased moment arm and less stress on the lumbar region. Consequently, individuals with lower back issues may find the Sumo Deadlift to be a more suitable option for heavy lifting.

Furthermore, the Sumo Deadlift places greater emphasis on the quadriceps and adductors, which can be advantageous for lifters with relatively stronger lower body muscles compared to their posterior chain. Additionally, the Sumo Deadlift allows for a shorter range of motion, which may benefit individuals with mobility limitations or those recovering from injuries.

Challenges and Considerations

While the Sumo Deadlift presents numerous advantages, it is not without its challenges. A common concern is the difficulty in finding the ideal stance width and foot positioning for each lifter. This can vary based on factors such as individual anatomy, mobility, and lifting experience. It is essential for lifters to experiment and fine-tune their setup to achieve optimal performance and avoid potential injury.

Another consideration is the grip variation used during the Sumo Deadlift. Some lifters prefer a double overhand grip, while others find a mixed grip (one hand pronated, one hand supinated) to be more secure. Grip strength can be a limiting factor in heavy lifting, so lifters must train their grip accordingly to ensure a secure and stable hold on the barbell.

As with any complex exercise, proper form, technique, and gradual progression are imperative to ensure safety and long-term progress. By incorporating the Sumo Deadlift into their training routines and honing their skills through consistent practice, lifters can unlock their true potential, unleashing the full power of the Sumo Deadlift to achieve greater strength and overall physical prowess.

Sumo Unlocked: Mastering the Art of the Sumo Deadlift

The Sumo Deadlift stands as an esteemed and potent lift, revered for its ability to recruit an array of muscle groups, culminating in a symphony of power and strength. Understanding the intricate interplay of these muscles during the Sumo Deadlift is essential to mastering this art and harnessing its true potential. In this essay, we shall delve into the depths of the muscles involved in the Sumo Deadlift, unraveling the complexity that underscores this formidable lift.

Muscles Involved in the Sumo Deadlift

The Sumo Deadlift is a multi-joint, compound exercise that engages various muscle groups synergistically to execute a successful lift. Central to this lift are the muscles of the lower body, including the quadriceps, adductors, hamstrings, glutes, and calves. Each muscle group plays a pivotal role in contributing to the force generation and stability required for a proficient Sumo Deadlift.

- **Quadriceps (Rectus Femoris, Vastus Medialis, Vastus Lateralis, Vastus Intermedius):** The quadriceps muscles, located in the front of the thigh, are heavily engaged during the initial phase of the lift. As the lifter begins to ascend from the starting position, the quadriceps contract forcefully to extend the knee joint. This extension action is fundamental to the initiation of the lift, providing the necessary force to overcome the resistance of the barbell.

- **Adductors (Adductor Magnus, Adductor Longus, Adductor Brevis, Gracilis, Pectineus):** Positioned on the inside of the thigh, the adductors play a critical role in stabilizing the pelvis and maintaining proper alignment during the Sumo Deadlift. These muscles assist in the initial phase of the lift, aiding the quadriceps in initiating the upward movement of the barbell.

- **Hamstrings (Biceps Femoris, Semitendinosus, Semimembranosus):** Situated at the back of the thigh, the hamstrings are integral to the Sumo Deadlift, as they contribute to both knee and hip extension. As the lifter rises from the initial position, the hamstrings contract powerfully to extend the hips, working in conjunction with the glutes to propel the body and the barbell upward.

- **Gluteus Maximus:** As the largest muscle in the gluteal group, the gluteus maximus plays a central role in hip extension during the Sumo Deadlift. This powerful muscle fires to drive the hips forward and maintain an upright torso position throughout the lift. The gluteus maximus works in harmony with the hamstrings, generating significant force to hoist the barbell off the ground.

- **Calves (Gastrocnemius, Soleus):** While not the primary movers in the Sumo Deadlift, the calf muscles play a supportive role in the lift. They aid in maintaining stability and balance by providing a strong base for the lifter's stance, especially during the initial setup and subsequent ascent.

- **Erector Spinae:** The erector spinae muscles, which consist of the iliocostalis, longissimus, and spinalis muscles, run along the length of the spine and play a crucial role in spinal extension. During the Sumo Deadlift, these muscles contract to maintain an upright and stable back position, preventing excessive flexion or rounding of the spine, which could lead to injury.

Synergy and Synchronization

The beauty of the Sumo Deadlift lies in the intricate synergy and synchronization of these muscle groups. As the lifter initiates the ascent, the quadriceps, adductors, and hamstrings work in concert to extend the knees and hips, propelling the body and the barbell upward. The glutes, acting as powerful extensors, drive the hips forward, while the erector spinae muscles maintain a rigid and neutral spine position, ensuring optimal force transfer throughout the lift.

To achieve maximum efficiency and effectiveness, lifters must focus on developing strength and coordination among these muscle groups. This can be accomplished through targeted strength training, emphasizing exercises that isolate and strengthen each muscle involved in the Sumo Deadlift. Additionally, practicing the Sumo Deadlift with proper form and technique is vital to ingraining the correct movement patterns and promoting muscle memory.

Mastering the Sumo Deadlift requires dedication, discipline, and a meticulous approach to training. By honing the strength and coordination of the muscles involved, lifters can unlock the true potential of this formidable lift, propelling themselves to new heights of strength and prowess in their pursuit of excellence.

Sumo Unlocked: Mastering the Art of the Sumo Deadlift

The Sumo Deadlift, a formidable and revered lift in the realm of strength training, has garnered attention for its unique approach and impressive benefits. However, like any exercise, the Sumo Deadlift is not without its limitations. Understanding the distinct advantages and inherent constraints of this lift is essential for lifters seeking to unlock its full potential. In this essay, we shall explore the benefits and limitations of the Sumo Deadlift, shedding light on the intricacies that govern this powerful art.

Benefits of the Sumo Deadlift

1. **Reduced Strain on the Lower Back:** One of the most significant advantages of the Sumo Deadlift lies in its reduced strain on the lower back compared to the conventional deadlift. The wider stance and grip placement inside the knees allow for a more upright torso position during the lift. This, in turn, results in a shorter moment arm around the lumbar spine, reducing the stress on the lower back. As a result, individuals with a history of lower back issues may find the Sumo Deadlift to be a more suitable option for heavy lifting, promoting safer training practices.

2. **Increased Quadriceps Engagement:** The Sumo Deadlift places greater emphasis on the quadriceps, the muscles located on the front of the thigh. The wider stance necessitates a more pronounced knee extension, requiring the quadriceps to work more intensely to initiate the lift. This increased quadriceps engagement can benefit lifters who possess relatively stronger lower body muscles compared to their posterior chain, enabling them to capitalize on their strengths during the lift.

3. **Shorter Range of Motion:** Unlike the conventional deadlift, which requires the hands to grip the barbell outside the knees and the feet to be placed shoulder-width apart, the Sumo Deadlift entails a wider stance and hand placement within the knees. This setup results in a shorter range of motion for the lift, making it an advantageous option for individuals with mobility limitations or those recovering from injuries. The reduced range

7

of motion can also contribute to a more efficient lift, conserving energy for heavier loads.

Limitations of the Sumo Deadlift

1. **Individual Biomechanics:** The Sumo Deadlift's effectiveness can be greatly influenced by an individual's biomechanics and body proportions. Some lifters may struggle to find the ideal stance width and foot positioning that suits their unique anatomy. Moreover, certain individuals with longer torsos or shorter arms may face challenges in maintaining an upright torso position during the lift, potentially compromising their performance.

2. **Grip Strength:** The Sumo Deadlift places significant demands on grip strength, especially when lifting heavy loads. Unlike the mixed grip commonly used in the conventional deadlift, the Sumo Deadlift typically employs a double overhand grip, which may be less secure for heavier weights. As such, lifters must dedicate attention to grip-specific training to ensure a firm and reliable grip on the barbell.

3. **Specificity for Other Lifts:** While the Sumo Deadlift is an exceptional lift on its own, its movement pattern and muscle recruitment differ from other strength exercises, such as the conventional deadlift and Olympic lifts. For athletes or lifters training for specific sports or competitions, the carryover of strength and skills from the Sumo Deadlift to other lifts may not be as pronounced. In such cases, a more comprehensive training approach that includes a variety of lifts may be necessary to meet their performance goals.

To master the art of the Sumo Deadlift, lifters must diligently address these limitations while capitalizing on its benefits. Proper form, targeted training, and gradual progression are crucial elements in optimizing performance and ensuring safety during the lift. By embracing a holistic approach to strength training, lifters can unlock the full potential of the Sumo Deadlift, harnessing its power to elevate their fitness journey to new heights of success and accomplishment.

Ethan R. Reynolds

CHAPTER 2: SETTING UP FOR SUCCESS

A crucial aspect of setting up for success in the Sumo Deadlift is finding the ideal stance width. In this chapter, we shall delve into the intricacies of this critical component, exploring the factors that influence stance width and the profound impact it has on the lift.

Finding Your Ideal Stance Width

The Sumo Deadlift is characterized by its wide stance, with the feet positioned significantly wider than shoulder-width apart. This setup sets the stage for an efficient and powerful lift, as it maximizes the lifter's mechanical advantage and leverage. However, determining the ideal stance width is not a one-size-fits-all endeavor; it is a highly individualized process that depends on several factors.

Factor 1: Hip Mobility

One of the primary considerations when selecting a stance width for the Sumo Deadlift is hip mobility.

Adequate hip mobility is essential for achieving proper depth and maintaining an upright torso during the lift. Lifters with greater hip mobility can often adopt a wider stance, allowing for deeper squatting positions and facilitating a more advantageous starting position. Conversely, individuals with limited hip mobility may find a slightly narrower stance to be more comfortable and manageable.

Factor 2: Anthropometry

Anthropometric measurements, such as leg length, torso length, and arm length, play a significant role in determining the optimal stance width for the Sumo Deadlift. Lifters with longer legs may benefit from a wider stance to reduce the range of motion required to lift the barbell. Similarly, individuals with shorter torsos may find a wider stance more conducive to maintaining an upright and stable back position throughout the lift. Experimenting with different stance widths can help lifters identify the configuration that best complements their unique body proportions.

Factor 3: Conventional Deadlift Background

Lifters who are transitioning from the conventional deadlift to the Sumo Deadlift may find that their previous lifting experiences influence their stance width preferences. Those accustomed to a narrower stance in the conventional deadlift may initially gravitate toward a narrower Sumo Deadlift stance as well. However, gradually widening the stance and adapting to the nuances of the Sumo Deadlift can lead to improved performance and greater benefits unique to this lift.

Factor 4: Training Goals

Individual training goals also warrant consideration

when determining the ideal stance width for the Sumo Deadlift. Lifters seeking to maximize their pulling strength and power may opt for a wider stance to leverage their strong lower body muscles effectively. Conversely, those aiming to build hypertrophy and muscle mass might prefer a narrower stance to emphasize the quadriceps and target specific muscle groups more directly.

Experimentation and Individualization

In essence, finding the ideal stance width for the Sumo Deadlift is a process of experimentation and individualization. Lifters must be willing to explore different configurations, making incremental adjustments to assess how each stance width impacts their performance. Recording and analyzing their lifts can provide valuable insights into the effectiveness of various setups, guiding them toward the stance width that optimizes their lifting capabilities.

Stance Width and Foot Positioning

While the focus of this essay is on finding the ideal stance width, it is important to recognize that foot positioning also plays a crucial role in the Sumo Deadlift setup. In addition to the width, the angle at which the feet are turned outward can influence the lifter's comfort, stability, and overall performance.

A common starting point for foot positioning is to angle the feet outward at approximately 45 degrees. This position allows the knees to track over the toes, facilitating a more natural and stable movement pattern during the lift. However, like stance width, foot positioning can also be adjusted based on individual preferences and anatomical considerations.

A well-chosen stance width in the Sumo Deadlift sets the stage for a powerful and efficient lift, enhancing mechanical advantage and leverage. By honing this crucial aspect of the Sumo Deadlift and complementing it with proper foot positioning, lifters can unlock the full potential of this formidable lift, forging a path towards mastering the art of the Sumo Deadlift and achieving greatness in their strength training journey.

In the realm of strength training, the Sumo Deadlift stands as an exceptional and revered lift, celebrated for its distinct approach and the immense power it bestows upon lifters. However, the mastery of this art extends beyond the execution of the lift itself, encompassing the meticulous details of the setup. A crucial component of setting up for success in the Sumo Deadlift lies in the selection of an appropriate grip variation. In this essay, we shall explore the significance of grip variations for the Sumo Deadlift, unveiling the nuances that govern this pivotal aspect of the lift.

The Importance of Grip Variations

The Sumo Deadlift, characterized by its wide stance and grip placement inside the knees, demands careful consideration of grip variations. The grip is the lifter's direct connection to the barbell, and it plays a critical role in maintaining control, stability, and lifting efficiency throughout the movement. Selecting the most suitable grip variation is integral to optimizing performance and reaping the full benefits of the Sumo Deadlift.

Grip Variation 1: Double Overhand Grip

The double overhand grip, as the name suggests,

involves placing both hands over the barbell with the palms facing the lifter and the thumbs wrapping around the bar. This grip variation is often the default choice for lifters, especially during lighter or moderate loads. It offers several advantages, including balanced muscle activation, reduced risk of imbalances, and a consistent grip experience.

However, the double overhand grip does have limitations, particularly when confronted with heavier weights. As the barbell load increases, grip strength becomes a limiting factor, and the likelihood of grip fatigue rises. As a result, lifters may find it challenging to maintain a secure hold on the bar throughout the entirety of the lift.

Grip Variation 2: Mixed Grip

The mixed grip, also known as the over-under grip, entails placing one hand in an overhand position (palm facing the lifter) and the other hand in an underhand position (palm facing away from the lifter). The mixed grip is a popular choice for lifters when handling heavier loads, as it significantly enhances grip strength and stability.

The mixed grip effectively counteracts the limitations of the double overhand grip, as it resists barbell rotation and minimizes the risk of the bar slipping out of the lifter's hands. This grip variation empowers lifters to lift heavier weights with greater confidence, allowing them to focus on the lift's execution and form without being constrained by grip fatigue.

Grip Variation 3: Hook Grip

The hook grip is a formidable grip variation utilized by many seasoned strength athletes. It involves wrapping the thumb under the fingers and securing it against the barbell. While the hook grip can be initially uncomfortable and challenging to master, it offers unparalleled grip strength and security.

One of the key advantages of the hook grip is its ability to prevent the barbell from rotating within the hands, providing an exceptionally strong hold throughout the lift. This grip variation is particularly popular among Olympic weightlifters, as it enables them to maintain a secure grip during explosive movements, such as the clean and snatch.

Grip Variation 4: Straps

Straps, or lifting straps, are an auxiliary tool that lifters can use to assist with their grip. Straps consist of durable material, such as nylon or leather, that wraps around the lifter's wrists and the barbell. When properly used, straps can help lifters hold onto the bar when grip strength becomes a limiting factor.

While straps offer undeniable advantages in terms of grip assistance, their usage can also be a double-edged sword. Relying too heavily on straps may hinder the development of natural grip strength, potentially leading to a dependency on the tool. As such, lifters should use straps judiciously and incorporate grip-specific training to continue building their grip strength.

Personalization and Progression

Selecting the most appropriate grip variation for the Sumo Deadlift is a highly individualized process that depends on factors such as lifting experience, grip strength, and training goals. Novice lifters or those with limited grip strength may find that the double overhand grip suffices for lighter loads and early stages of training. As they progress and encounter heavier weights, exploring the mixed grip or the hook grip can be beneficial in enhancing lifting capabilities.

Furthermore, it is essential for lifters to continuously challenge their grip strength through targeted training and progressive overload. This can involve performing accessory exercises, such as farmer's walks or plate pinches, to fortify the hands and forearms. Developing a robust grip strength not only enhances performance in the Sumo Deadlift but also translates to improvements in various other lifting exercises.

As lifters progress in their strength training journey, the mastery of various grip variations and the continual development of grip strength become essential components in unlocking the true potential of the Sumo Deadlift. By fine-tuning their grip technique and adopting a strategic approach to grip-specific training, lifters can truly master the art of the Sumo Deadlift, propelling themselves to unparalleled levels of strength and accomplishment.

A pivotal aspect of setting up for success in the Sumo Deadlift lies in the deliberate consideration of foot positioning and angle. In this essay, we shall explore the profound significance of these critical elements, illuminating the subtleties that govern the foot placement in the Sumo Deadlift.

Foot Positioning: The Foundation of Stability

At the heart of the Sumo Deadlift lies the establishment of a solid foundation through foot positioning. The positioning of the feet not only influences the lifter's stability but also determines the mechanics and force distribution throughout the lift. The art of foot positioning is a nuanced endeavor that involves careful calibration of stance width, foot angle, and weight distribution.

Stance Width: Striking the Right Balance

The Sumo Deadlift is characterized by its wide stance, with the feet positioned substantially wider than shoulder-width apart. The selection of the optimal stance width is a critical factor in achieving the desired balance of mobility and stability.

A stance that is too narrow may restrict hip mobility and hinder the lifter's ability to attain proper depth. On the other hand, an excessively wide stance may compromise the lifter's stability and impede an efficient upward drive during the lift.

Individual factors such as hip mobility, anthropometry, and personal comfort influence the ideal stance width. Lifters must consider their anatomical proportions and experiment with varying widths to discover the configuration that best suits their unique physique and mechanics.

Foot Angle: Precision and Positioning

Foot angle, or the degree to which the feet are turned outward, is another crucial element in the Sumo Deadlift setup. The appropriate foot angle influences the lifter's ability to engage specific muscle groups and maintain proper alignment throughout the lift.

An outward foot angle allows for optimal engagement of the adductors and provides a stable platform for the ascent. However, excessive foot turnout may place undue stress on the knees and compromise the lifter's ability to generate force effectively.

Conversely, insufficient foot turnout may impede the lifter's ability to track the knees over the toes, leading to an unstable and less powerful lift.

Finding the Perfect Balance

Achieving the perfect balance in foot angle is a delicate process that requires thoughtful experimentation and fine-tuning. Lifters should aim to find the degree of foot turnout that allows for comfortable knee tracking while minimizing unnecessary strain on the joints.

The sumo stance typically involves an outward foot angle ranging from 30 to 45 degrees. However, personal preference and individual biomechanics may lead some lifters to adopt slightly greater or lesser angles.

Weight Distribution: Striking the Ground with Precision

In the Sumo Deadlift, the weight distribution between the feet is integral to achieving a solid foundation and generating maximal force. A balanced weight distribution ensures that the lifter's power is evenly distributed through both legs, facilitating a symmetrical and efficient lift.

Lifters should strive to maintain an even distribution of weight between the balls of the feet and the heels. Placing too much weight on the toes may cause the lifter to lean forward excessively, compromising the lift's mechanical advantage and leading to reduced stability. Conversely, shifting too much weight onto the heels may result in an overly vertical torso position, potentially leading to a loss of balance and power.

Positioning for Success

The Sumo Deadlift setup is a meticulous process that culminates in positioning the feet with precision. By adhering to the principles of stance width, foot angle, and weight distribution, lifters create the optimal conditions for a powerful and efficient lift.

Footwear Considerations

Footwear plays a significant role in the Sumo Deadlift setup, directly impacting foot positioning, stability, and force transfer. Lifters often opt for shoes with flat, non-compressible soles, which provide a stable platform for lifting. This allows for maximum ground contact and enhances the lifter's ability to generate force through the feet.

Lifting in shoes with excessive cushioning or elevated heels may disrupt the lifter's center of gravity, impeding proper weight distribution and stability. Additionally, the use of shoes with raised heels may alter the lifter's foot angle, affecting muscle engagement and the mechanics of the lift.

Lifters must consider their individual anatomy, mobility, and biomechanics when determining the most suitable foot positioning for the Sumo Deadlift. By striving for balance and precision in the setup, lifters unlock the potential for a powerful and efficient lift, propelling themselves towards mastery of the art of the Sumo Deadlift and the realization of their strength training aspirations.

Ethan R. Reynolds

CHAPTER 3: PERFECTING YOUR FORM

The Sumo Deadlift, an eminent and revered lift in the realm of strength training, demands not only sheer power but also meticulous attention to form. Perfecting the form of the Sumo Deadlift is a relentless pursuit, and two key components that warrant unwavering focus are hip and shoulder positioning. In this chapter, we shall delve into the profound significance of these critical elements, unveiling the intricate mechanics that underpin the proper hip and shoulder positioning in the Sumo Deadlift.

Hip Positioning: The Foundation of Power

The hip position in the Sumo Deadlift serves as the foundation upon which the lift's force and stability are built. Optimal hip positioning is paramount in facilitating a powerful and efficient lift, while simultaneously mitigating the risk of injury. The intricacies of hip positioning are influenced by various factors, including mobility, anatomical proportions, and individual biomechanics.

Initiating the Lift: The Hip Hinge

A fundamental aspect of hip positioning in the Sumo Deadlift is the initiation of the lift through a controlled hip hinge. The hip hinge is a vital movement pattern that allows the lifter to engage the posterior chain effectively. As the lifter approaches the barbell, they must bend at the hips while maintaining a straight and neutral spine, ensuring that the weight is distributed over the midfoot.

The hip hinge not only optimizes force generation but also protects the lower back from excessive stress. A well-executed hip hinge enables the lifter to engage the glutes, hamstrings, and erector spinae in a coordinated manner, setting the stage for a powerful and stable ascent.

Depth and Torso Position

Another key consideration in hip positioning is the depth achieved during the lift and the accompanying torso position. The depth attained in the Sumo Deadlift may vary depending on individual mobility and anatomical factors. Lifters should aim to find a depth that allows for an effective hip hinge while maintaining a neutral spine and proper alignment.

Excessive depth may lead to a rounded back, compromising the lifter's stability and potentially increasing the risk of injury. Conversely, inadequate depth may hinder the lifter's ability to generate maximal force and power through the hips.

Achieving the appropriate depth requires practice, awareness, and flexibility. Lifters should engage in regular mobility work to enhance hip and hamstring flexibility, facilitating an optimal range of motion for the lift.

The Importance of Hip Drive

Hip drive is a critical component of hip positioning in the Sumo Deadlift. As the lifter ascends from the starting position, they must drive the hips forward forcefully, engaging the glutes and hamstrings to generate upward force. The hip drive is instrumental in overcoming the initial resistance of the barbell and propelling the weight to an upright position.

Proper hip drive involves a coordinated effort between the lower body and the core. As the hips extend, the lifter should simultaneously engage the core muscles to maintain a stable and neutral spine, avoiding any hyperextension or excessive arching of the lower back.

Shoulder Positioning: Stability and Alignment

In addition to hip positioning, the alignment and stability of the shoulders play a crucial role in perfecting the form of the Sumo Deadlift. Correct shoulder positioning not only enhances lifting efficiency but also safeguards against potential shoulder injuries.

Hand Placement and Grip Width

The position of the hands and the grip width are central to shoulder positioning in the Sumo Deadlift. As the lifter sets up to grip the barbell, the hands should be positioned inside the knees, enabling the arms to align with the torso. The grip width may vary depending on individual comfort and preference, but lifters typically opt for a grip that allows for adequate clearance between the knees and the arms during the lift.

Retracting the Scapulae

Before initiating the lift, lifters should focus on retracting the scapulae or pulling the shoulder blades back and down. This action stabilizes the shoulders and engages the upper back muscles, creating a solid foundation for the lift. Proper scapular retraction contributes to improved force transfer and reduces the risk of shoulder impingement during the movement.

Maintaining Neutral Shoulders

Throughout the lift, it is imperative for lifters to maintain neutral shoulders. Any excessive protraction or rounding of the shoulders can compromise stability and diminish force generation. Lifters should strive to keep the shoulders in line with the hips and maintain a tight upper back to ensure a strong and stable position throughout the ascent.

The pursuit of mastery in the Sumo Deadlift demands dedication, practice, and a relentless commitment to refining form and technique. By honing the intricacies of hip and shoulder positioning, lifters unlock the true potential of this formidable lift, propelling themselves towards the artful and powerful execution of the Sumo Deadlift and elevating their strength training journey to new heights of accomplishment.

The Sumo Deadlift stands as an eminent and revered lift, celebrated for its unique approach and the immense power it bestows upon those who conquer it. Yet, the true mastery of this art extends beyond raw strength; it resides in the precision and finesse of perfecting form. Key to this endeavor is the unwavering focus on back and core engagement.

Back Engagement: The Pillar of Stability

The role of back engagement in the Sumo Deadlift cannot be overstated. A strong and stable back not only ensures safe execution but also maximizes force transfer throughout the lift. Proper back engagement begins with understanding the role of various muscle groups and the importance of maintaining a neutral spine.

Erector Spinae: The Back's Support System

The erector spinae muscles, located along the length of the spine, serve as the primary support system for the back during the Sumo Deadlift. These muscles play a pivotal role in maintaining an upright and neutral spine position, ensuring that the load is distributed evenly along the vertebral column.

Engaging the erector spinae is a two-fold process. As the lifter approaches the barbell, they must brace their core and simultaneously contract the erector spinae to stabilize the spine. This protective mechanism safeguards against excessive flexion or rounding of the back, mitigating the risk of injury.

Upper Back Engagement: The Scapular Retractors

Scapular retractors, including the rhomboids and middle trapezius, contribute to the engagement of the upper back during the Sumo Deadlift. By pulling the shoulder blades back and down, lifters establish a stable foundation for the lift and prevent the shoulders from rounding forward. Proper upper back engagement enhances force transfer through the upper body and enables the lifter to maintain a tight and controlled form.

Core Engagement: The Center of Power

An active and resilient core serves as the center of power in the Sumo Deadlift. Core engagement is instrumental in creating intra-abdominal pressure, enhancing stability, and facilitating force transfer from the lower body to the upper body.

Creating Intra-Abdominal Pressure: The Valsalva Maneuver

One of the fundamental principles of core engagement in the Sumo Deadlift is the utilization of the Valsalva maneuver. The Valsalva maneuver involves taking a deep breath and holding it while simultaneously bracing the abdominal muscles. This action increases intra-abdominal pressure, which acts as a natural weightlifting belt, supporting the spine and enhancing lifting performance.

The Valsalva maneuver not only enhances back stability but also reduces the risk of injury by preventing excessive spine flexion. Lifters should practice this technique to effectively harness the power of their core during the Sumo Deadlift.

Transverse Abdominis: The Deep Core Stabilizer

The transverse abdominis, often referred to as the body's natural weight belt, plays a crucial role in core stability during the Sumo Deadlift. This deep-lying muscle acts as a corset, providing support to the spine and pelvis.

To engage the transverse abdominis, lifters can focus on drawing their belly button in towards their spine while maintaining the Valsalva maneuver. This action creates a strong and stable core foundation, further reinforcing the integrity of the lift.

Obliques: The Twisting Stabilizers

The obliques, located on the sides of the torso, serve as dynamic stabilizers during the Sumo Deadlift. These muscles play a significant role in counteracting rotational forces, maintaining an aligned and controlled lift.

To engage the obliques effectively, lifters can focus on tightening their sides and resisting any twisting or tilting movements during the lift. This engagement contributes to the overall stability and precision of the Sumo Deadlift.

Coordination of Back and Core Engagement

The interplay of back and core engagement is a symphony of strength, requiring coordination and synchronization of various muscle groups. As the lifter approaches the barbell, they must initiate the hip hinge while simultaneously engaging the back and core muscles. This coordinated effort creates a harmonious balance of stability and power throughout the lift.

Perfecting Form: The Art of Mastery

The pursuit of perfecting form in the Sumo Deadlift is an art that demands relentless dedication and attention to detail. Lifters must be attuned to their body mechanics, continually refining back and core engagement through deliberate practice and self-awareness.

Regular strength training, including exercises that target the erector spinae, upper back, and core muscles, can bolster back and core strength. Furthermore, incorporating accessory exercises, such as planks and bird-dogs, can refine the nuances of back and core engagement specific to the Sumo Deadlift.

The pursuit of perfection in the Sumo Deadlift requires unwavering commitment and a profound understanding of the intricacies of back and core engagement. By honing these critical elements, lifters unlock the true potential of this formidable lift, transcending mere strength to achieve the artful and powerful execution of the Sumo Deadlift.

Knee Positioning: The Gateway to Power and Stability

The positioning of the knees in the Sumo Deadlift is a cornerstone of power and stability. Proper knee alignment is vital in optimizing force transfer and safeguarding against potential injury. Understanding the intricacies of knee positioning is crucial for achieving an efficient and powerful lift.

Knee Tracking: Maintaining the Line

One of the primary considerations in knee positioning is the concept of knee tracking. Proper knee tracking involves ensuring that the knees align with the toes throughout the entire movement. As the lifter descends to grip the barbell, the knees should track outward in line with the feet's direction, promoting an efficient and stable lift.

Inadequate knee tracking, such as knees caving inward, can lead to compromised force transfer and increased stress on the knee joint. By actively engaging the hip abductors and external rotators, lifters can maintain proper knee alignment, optimizing the lift's mechanical advantage and minimizing the risk of injury.

Knee Flexion: Striking the Right Balance

The degree of knee flexion, or how much the knees are bent, is another critical aspect of knee positioning in the Sumo Deadlift. Striking the right balance of knee flexion is essential in achieving an optimal starting position and generating maximum power during the ascent.

Excessive knee flexion may lead to an overly squat-like stance, limiting the lifter's ability to hinge at the hips and engage the posterior chain effectively. On the other hand, insufficient knee flexion may hinder the lifter's ability to lower down to the barbell and engage the quads and glutes in the initial phase of the lift.

Lifters should experiment with varying degrees of knee flexion to find the stance that allows for an effective hip hinge while still enabling proper depth and power generation.

Shin Positioning: The Path to Efficient Force Transfer

The position of the shins in the Sumo Deadlift is a critical determinant of force transfer and lift efficiency. Proper shin positioning maximizes the contribution of the lower body muscles and ensures a smooth and powerful ascent.

Shin Angle: Finding the Sweet Spot

The angle at which the shins are positioned relative to the floor is a key consideration in the Sumo Deadlift. The ideal shin angle will vary depending on individual mobility, stance width, and anatomical proportions.

A more vertical shin angle allows for greater engagement of the posterior chain, emphasizing the glutes and hamstrings during the lift. A more horizontal shin angle places greater emphasis on the quads and quadriceps, enhancing force production from the lower body.

The lifter's unique mechanics and training objectives will influence the optimal shin angle. Lifters should explore different angles and find the sweet spot that allows for effective force transfer and muscle engagement.

Shin Verticality: Balancing Hip Hinge and Knee Flexion

A key consideration in shin positioning is maintaining verticality relative to the floor while striking a balance between hip hinge and knee flexion. As the lifter initiates the lift, the shins should remain as vertical as possible to optimize force transfer through the posterior chain.

As the barbell ascends, lifters must continue to balance the hip hinge with knee extension. Avoiding excessive forward shin movement can ensure that the lifter effectively utilizes the force generated from the hips and legs to propel the barbell upward.

Coordination of Knees and Shins: The Synchronization of Power

The coordination of knees and shins in the Sumo Deadlift is a symphony of power, requiring precise timing and movement. As the lifter descends to grip the barbell, the knees should track outward while the shins maintain verticality, setting the stage for a powerful hip hinge.

Throughout the ascent, lifters must maintain proper knee alignment and shin positioning, allowing for efficient force transfer and muscle engagement. The synchronization of these elements is instrumental in achieving a smooth and powerful lift.

Understanding the nuances of knee and shin mechanics empowers lifters to unlock the true potential of this formidable lift, transcending mere strength to achieve the artful and powerful execution of the Sumo Deadlift.

Ethan R. Reynolds

CHAPTER 4: EXECUTING THE LIFT

Among the myriad components that contribute to its mastery, the pulling sequence takes center stage. The pulling sequence in the Sumo Deadlift involves a precise and coordinated series of movements that culminate in a powerful and fluid ascent. We shall explore the profound significance of the pulling sequence, unveiling the intricacies that underpin the art of executing the Sumo Deadlift with precision and finesse.

The Setup: Laying the Foundation

The pulling sequence commences with the lifter's setup, a crucial phase that establishes the foundation for a successful lift. As the lifter approaches the barbell, they position themselves with a wide stance, feet outside shoulder-width, and toes pointed slightly outward. The hands grip the barbell inside the knees, and the back remains straight, maintaining a neutral spine.

Engaging the back and core muscles, the lifter takes a deep breath and performs the Valsalva maneuver, creating intra-abdominal pressure to stabilize the spine. Scapular retractors are engaged, pulling the shoulder blades back and down, establishing a stable and aligned upper body.

The Initial Pull: Harnessing the Power of the Hips

The first phase of the pulling sequence involves the initial pull, where the lifter engages the powerful hip extensor muscles to break the barbell off the ground. With the back and core engaged, the lifter drives through the heels, pushing the floor away with forceful hip extension.

The hip hinge is the focal point of this phase, ensuring that the lift's initiation comes from the posterior chain, specifically the glutes and hamstrings. The lifter maintains a vertical shin angle, allowing for efficient force transfer and power generation through the lower body.

The Knees and Shins: Coordinated Movement

As the barbell rises off the ground, the pulling sequence demands a coordinated movement of the knees and shins. The knees track outward in line with the toes, maintaining proper knee alignment throughout the lift. Simultaneously, the shins remain as vertical as possible, ensuring efficient force transfer through the posterior chain.

Coordinating the movement of the knees and shins optimizes the lifter's power output and minimizes the risk of injury. A smooth and synchronous motion of these elements establishes the groundwork for a fluid and powerful ascent.

The Lockout: The Culmination of Strength

The culmination of the pulling sequence lies in the lockout phase, where the lifter stands tall, fully extending the hips and knees to complete the lift. As the barbell reaches the top position, the lifter maintains a tight and engaged upper body, with the shoulder blades pulled back and down, and the core braced.

In this final phase, the lifter achieves full extension of the hips, ensuring that the body forms a straight line from head to heel. The glutes and lower back muscles play a pivotal role in achieving this alignment, solidifying the lockout and showcasing the lifter's strength and control.

The Descent: Controlled and Deliberate

The pulling sequence is not complete without the controlled descent of the barbell. As the lifter lowers the weight, they maintain an engaged and stable upper body, ensuring that the spine remains neutral throughout the descent.

The hips hinge back, guiding the barbell downward while the knees and shins coordinate their movement to maintain proper alignment. The lifter must resist the urge to rush the descent, maintaining control and balance until the barbell returns to the ground.

Muscle Engagement: The Symphony of Strength

Throughout the pulling sequence, various muscle groups harmonize to form a symphony of strength. The glutes, hamstrings, quads, and erector spinae in the posterior chain work in unison to drive the lift off the ground and maintain the necessary force throughout the ascent.

The quadriceps, along with the hip abductors and external rotators, play a critical role in knee tracking and stability. The core muscles, including the transverse abdominis and obliques, provide a solid foundation for force transfer and protect the spine.

Fine-Tuning the Pulling Sequence: The Art of Mastery

The mastery of the pulling sequence in the Sumo Deadlift demands dedication, practice, and a profound understanding of the body's mechanics. Lifters must be attuned to their individual biomechanics, continually refining the pulling sequence through deliberate practice and self-awareness.

Regular strength training, including exercises that target the posterior chain and core, can bolster the necessary muscle engagement for a powerful pull. Additionally, incorporating accessory exercises, such as Romanian deadlifts and hip thrusts, can refine the nuances of the pulling sequence specific to the Sumo Deadlift.

Throughout the sequence, various muscle groups work in harmony to create a symphony of strength, propelling the lifter towards mastery of the art of the Sumo Deadlift. Through dedicated practice and an unwavering commitment to perfecting the pulling sequence, lifters unlock the true potential of this formidable lift, elevating their strength training journey to new heights of accomplishment.

The Sumo Deadlift, revered and admired in the realm of

strength training, demands not only raw power but also a profound understanding of the subtleties that govern its execution. Among the myriad factors that contribute to its mastery, breathing techniques stand as a pivotal element. Proper breathing during the Sumo Deadlift is integral to optimizing performance, enhancing stability, and safeguarding against potential injuries.

Breathing and Intra-Abdominal Pressure: The Foundation of Stability

At the core of breathing techniques for the Sumo Deadlift lies the concept of intra-abdominal pressure (IAP). IAP is the pressurization of the abdominal cavity, achieved by taking a deep breath and engaging the core muscles in a coordinated manner. This intra-abdominal pressure acts as a natural weightlifting belt, providing stability to the spine and pelvis during the lift.

The Valsalva Maneuver: Harnessing the Power of Pressure

One of the fundamental breathing techniques used in the Sumo Deadlift is the Valsalva maneuver. The Valsalva maneuver involves taking a deep breath into the belly while simultaneously bracing the core muscles. This action creates a high level of intra-abdominal pressure, akin to inflating a balloon within the abdomen.

Engaging in the Valsalva maneuver during the Sumo Deadlift ensures a rigid and stable core, effectively locking the spine in a neutral position. This stabilization protects the spine from excessive flexion or rounding during the lift, reducing the risk of injury and optimizing force transfer.

Breathing Rhythm: Timing the Inhale and Exhale

The execution of the Sumo Deadlift demands a specific breathing rhythm to optimize breath control and maintain IAP throughout the lift. The breathing rhythm generally follows a pattern of inhaling at the setup phase and exhaling during the lockout phase.

As the lifter approaches the barbell, they take a deep breath, expanding the belly to fill the lungs fully. This deep inhalation sets the stage for creating IAP and initiating the Valsalva maneuver.

As the lifter begins the pull and ascends from the ground, the exhalation commences. Exhaling during the exertion phase allows the lifter to maintain IAP while preventing excessive breath-holding, which can lead to decreased force output and reduced performance.

The Controlled Exhale: Managing Intra-Abdominal Pressure

While exhaling during the ascent is crucial to maintain IAP, lifters should be mindful of not exhaling rapidly or excessively. A controlled exhale ensures that the pressure in the abdomen remains constant and supportive throughout the lift.

Rapidly exhaling during the ascent may cause a loss of IAP and result in a weakened core, compromising stability and force generation. The goal is to exhale gradually and deliberately, managing IAP throughout the lift while harnessing the power of breath control.

The Breath Reset: Transitioning between Repetitions

In multiple-repetition sets of the Sumo Deadlift, a breath reset between repetitions is essential. After completing a lift, the lifter returns the barbell to the ground and takes a moment to reset the breath before initiating the next repetition.

The breath reset involves returning to the setup position, taking a deep breath, and re-engaging the core to create IAP. This brief pause allows the lifter to regain stability and prepare for the subsequent repetition, ensuring consistent and controlled breathing throughout the set.

Consistency and Mindfulness: Keys to Effective Breathing Techniques

Consistency and mindfulness are critical aspects of effective breathing techniques in the Sumo Deadlift. Lifters must practice breath control consistently in their training, making it a habit that translates seamlessly to heavier lifts and competition settings.

Mindful breathing fosters a deep mind-muscle connection, allowing lifters to be attuned to their body's responses and adjust their breathing rhythm accordingly. The lifter's ability to maintain IAP and control breath throughout the lift contributes to overall performance and ensures a safer and more efficient execution.

Incorporating Breathing Techniques into Training

Incorporating breathing techniques into training for the Sumo Deadlift involves deliberate practice and awareness. Lifters should focus on mastering the Valsalva maneuver and coordinating breath control with movement to optimize force transfer and stability.

Practicing breath resets between repetitions and during various set configurations allows lifters to fine-tune their breathing rhythm, preparing them for the demands of heavier lifts and competition scenarios.

A well-timed breathing rhythm, including the controlled exhale during the ascent and breath resets between repetitions, ensures consistency and stability throughout the lift. Incorporating breathing techniques into training establishes the foundation for mastery in the art of the Sumo Deadlift, empowering lifters to unlock their true potential and elevate their strength training journey to new heights of accomplishment.

The Sumo Deadlift, a revered and dynamic lift in the realm of strength training, demands not only raw power but also meticulous attention to form and technique. As lifters embark on the journey of mastering this formidable lift, they encounter various challenges and common mistakes that can hinder progress and compromise performance. In this essay, we shall explore the most prevalent mistakes made during the Sumo Deadlift and provide insightful guidance on how to correct them, unlocking the path to executing the lift with precision and finesse.

Mistake 1: Incorrect Foot Placement

One of the most common mistakes in the Sumo Deadlift is incorrect foot placement. If the feet are positioned too close together, lifters risk sacrificing stability and may struggle to engage the posterior chain effectively. Conversely, if the feet are too wide apart, the lifter may encounter difficulties in initiating the lift and maintaining proper alignment.

Correction: To address this issue, lifters should experiment with various foot widths during their warm-up sets. The ideal stance width will allow the lifter to maintain a vertical shin angle while engaging the hips and hamstrings effectively. A good starting point is to position the feet just outside shoulder-width and gradually adjust from there, finding the stance that best suits individual biomechanics and comfort.

Mistake 2: Rounded Back and Poor Hip Hinge

A rounded back and poor hip hinge are frequent errors in the Sumo Deadlift, leading to compromised form and an increased risk of lower back injuries. Lifting with a rounded back places excessive stress on the spinal discs and diminishes the engagement of powerful posterior chain muscles.

Correction: To correct this mistake, lifters should prioritize maintaining a neutral spine throughout the lift. Engaging the core and bracing the back will create a strong foundation for the lift. Initiating the movement with a controlled hip hinge and ensuring that the hips and shoulders rise simultaneously will help preserve proper alignment and optimize force transfer.

Mistake 3: Lack of Hip Drive

The absence of sufficient hip drive is another common pitfall in the Sumo Deadlift. Without proper hip drive, lifters may struggle to generate enough power to break the barbell off the ground, leading to inefficient lifts and missed opportunities to lift heavier weights.

Correction: To develop effective hip drive, lifters should focus on forcefully extending the hips during the ascent phase of the lift. Initiating the movement by pushing through the heels and actively engaging the glutes and hamstrings will facilitate a powerful hip drive, propelling the barbell upward.

Mistake 4: Inadequate Knee Tracking

Improper knee tracking is a prevalent mistake during the Sumo Deadlift, where the knees may cave inward or deviate from their intended path. This misalignment can reduce force transfer and increase the risk of knee-related injuries.

Correction: Lifters can correct inadequate knee tracking by consciously pushing the knees outward in line with the toes throughout the lift. Engaging the hip abductors and external rotators will assist in maintaining proper knee alignment, optimizing the lift's mechanical advantage.

Mistake 5: Poor Grip and Hand Placement

Poor grip and hand placement are detrimental to a successful Sumo Deadlift. An incorrect grip width or grip that is too narrow may limit the lifter's ability to create tension and leverage during the lift.

Correction: To address grip issues, lifters should experiment with different grip widths and find a position that allows for adequate clearance between the knees and the arms during the lift. The hands should be positioned inside the knees, and the grip should be firm and secure.

Mistake 6: Failure to Engage the Lats

The lats, essential muscles of the upper back, play a critical role in the Sumo Deadlift by stabilizing the spine and maintaining proper positioning throughout the lift. Failing to engage the lats may result in a compromised upper body and reduced stability.

Correction: Lifters should focus on retracting the scapulae, pulling the shoulder blades back and down, to effectively engage the lats. This action creates a stable platform for the upper body and enhances the lifter's ability to maintain a neutral spine.

Mistake 7: Neglecting Deliberate Breath Control

Ignoring proper breath control during the Sumo Deadlift can lead to diminished stability and reduced power output. Failing to use breathing techniques, such as the Valsalva maneuver, may result in a weakened core and compromised force transfer.

Correction: To optimize breath control, lifters should practice the Valsalva maneuver, taking a deep breath into the belly and bracing the core during the lift. This technique helps create intra-abdominal pressure, stabilizing the spine and safeguarding against injury.

Mistake 8: Rushing the Descent

Rushing the descent of the barbell is a common error that can disrupt proper form and compromise the lift's efficacy. A hasty descent may lead to loss of tension and control, negating the benefits of a well-executed pull.

Correction: Lifters should prioritize a controlled and deliberate descent of the barbell. Maintaining tension in the core and maintaining proper alignment during the lowering phase ensures a smooth and stable transition between repetitions.

Mistake 9: Overemphasizing Upper Body Pull

Overemphasizing the upper body pull, rather than relying on proper hip and leg drive, is a mistake that limits the lifter's potential to lift heavier weights. Relying too heavily on the arms and back may exhaust these muscle groups prematurely.

Correction: Lifters should focus on generating power from the hips and legs, employing the posterior chain to initiate and drive the lift. Engaging the glutes, hamstrings, and quads will distribute the workload more efficiently and enable the lifter to lift more substantial loads.

Mistake 10: Lack of Consistency in Practice

Finally, a lack of consistency in practice can hinder progress in mastering the Sumo Deadlift. Failing to practice regularly and neglecting deliberate refinement of technique may impede the development of strength and skill.

Correction: To overcome this mistake, lifters should prioritize consistent and intentional practice. Regularly incorporating the Sumo Deadlift into their training regimen and dedicating time to refine form and address weaknesses will accelerate progress towards mastery.

Prioritizing deliberate breath control, engaging the lats, and maintaining proper knee tracking further enhance form and stability. Regular practice and mindfulness in addressing these mistakes enable lifters to unlock the true potential of this formidable lift, elevating their strength training journey to new heights of accomplishment.

CHAPTER 5: TRAINING STRATEGIES

Mastering the art of the Sumo Deadlift requires more than mere physical prowess; it necessitates a well-structured and strategic training approach. Let us explore training strategies focused on incorporating the Sumo Deadlift into your routine, enabling lifters to harness the full potential of this dynamic lift while fostering balanced and well-rounded strength development.

1.   Assessing Readiness: Laying the Foundation

Before incorporating the Sumo Deadlift into your training routine, it is essential to assess your readiness and foundation in strength training. Beginners or individuals unfamiliar with deadlifting should first develop a solid foundation in conventional deadlifts or other compound exercises.

Conventional deadlifts build fundamental strength and familiarity with proper lifting mechanics, which can seamlessly translate into Sumo Deadlift execution. Once confident in your ability to perform conventional deadlifts with proper form, you can transition to incorporating Sumo Deadlifts into your routine.

2.   Gradual Progression: Emphasizing Technique

When introducing Sumo Deadlifts to your routine, emphasize gradual progression and focus on refining technique. Start with lighter weights to acclimate to the new movement pattern and reinforce proper form. Pay close attention to foot placement, hip hinge, knee tracking, and grip during the initial stages of incorporating Sumo Deadlifts.

As you become more comfortable with the lift, gradually increase the weight, ensuring that your form remains consistent. Utilizing video recordings of your lifts and seeking feedback from experienced coaches or training partners can aid in identifying areas for improvement and fine-tuning your technique.

3.   Targeted Accessory Exercises: Strengthening Weak Points

Incorporate targeted accessory exercises into your training to address specific weaknesses in the Sumo Deadlift. Strengthening the muscles involved in the Sumo Deadlift will not only enhance your performance but also reduce the risk of injury.

Accessory exercises such as Romanian deadlifts, glute bridges, and hip thrusts target the posterior chain, improving hip hinge mechanics and building strength in the glutes and hamstrings. Additionally, incorporating exercises that emphasize grip strength, such as farmer's walks or towel pull-ups, can bolster your grip for better barbell control in the Sumo Deadlift.

4. Variation and Periodization: Progressive Overload

Introduce variation and periodization into your training to facilitate progressive overload and prevent stagnation. Periodization involves organizing training into distinct phases, each with specific goals and training intensities.

During the preparatory phase, focus on technique refinement and lighter loads to build a solid foundation. As you progress to the strength-building phase, gradually increase the weight and intensity while maintaining proper form. The peaking phase should be characterized by higher intensity and lower volume, leading up to a planned peak performance in the Sumo Deadlift.

Variation can include altering foot placement, using different barbell heights, or implementing tempo training. These variations challenge the body in new ways, stimulate muscle adaptation, and promote continuous progress in the Sumo Deadlift.

5. Frequency and Recovery: Striking the Balance

Finding the optimal balance between training frequency and recovery is essential in incorporating the Sumo Deadlift into your routine. While frequency can stimulate muscle growth and strength gains, too much training without adequate recovery can lead to overtraining and potential injury.

Aim to deadlift with a frequency that allows for sufficient recovery between sessions. For some lifters, this may mean deadlifting once or twice a week, while others may benefit from less frequent sessions. Listen to your body and adjust your training schedule accordingly.

6. Balancing Movements: The Whole-Body Approach

The Sumo Deadlift is a potent lift that emphasizes the lower body and posterior chain. However, to foster a well-rounded strength development and prevent muscular imbalances, it is vital to balance your training with other compound movements.

Incorporate exercises such as squats, bench presses, overhead presses, and rows to engage different muscle groups and promote overall strength. A comprehensive training program that encompasses the whole body will contribute to greater stability and improved performance in the Sumo Deadlift.

7. Rest and Nutrition: Supporting Recovery and Growth

Adequate rest and nutrition play a significant role in supporting recovery and muscle growth during your Sumo Deadlift training. Ensure that you prioritize sufficient sleep and rest between training sessions to allow the body to repair and adapt to the demands of lifting.

Additionally, pay attention to your nutrition to provide your body with the fuel it needs to recover and grow stronger. Adequate protein intake, balanced macronutrients, and proper hydration are all crucial components of an effective training program.

8. Mindfulness and Patience: The Art of Mastery

Incorporating the Sumo Deadlift into your routine requires mindfulness and patience. Embrace the learning process and acknowledge that mastery takes time and dedication. Focus on each lift, pay attention to your body's responses, and celebrate incremental progress.

Be patient with yourself and recognize that improvement may come gradually. Trust the process, stay consistent with your training, and maintain a positive mindset.

Strike the balance between training frequency and recovery, complement Sumo Deadlifts with other compound movements, and prioritize rest and nutrition to support recovery and growth. Above all, approach the journey with mindfulness and patience, embracing the art of mastering the Sumo Deadlift.

As lifters seek to master the art of deadlifting, the question arises: Sumo Deadlift vs. Conventional Deadlift - which is right for you?

The Sumo Deadlift: Wide Stance, Efficient Pull

The Sumo Deadlift derives its name from the wide foot placement of the lifter, with feet positioned outside shoulder-width and toes angled outward. This wide stance allows the lifter to assume a more upright position during the lift, reducing the range of motion and placing greater emphasis on the lower body, particularly the hips and quadriceps.

Training Strategies for the Sumo Deadlift

1. **Emphasis on Leg Strength:** The Sumo Deadlift relies heavily on leg strength, particularly the adductors and quadriceps, to initiate the lift. Training strategies should include exercises that target these muscle groups, such as squats, leg presses, and lunges.

2. **Hip Mobility and Flexibility:** Sumo Deadlifts require adequate hip mobility and flexibility to assume the wide stance and maintain proper positioning. Incorporating hip mobility exercises, such as hip flexor stretches and dynamic warm-ups, can improve overall performance in the Sumo Deadlift.

3. **Grip Strength and Stability:** While the Sumo Deadlift places less demand on the lower back compared to the Conventional Deadlift, it places greater emphasis on grip strength and stability due to the wider hand placement. Accessory exercises such as farmer's walks and towel pull-ups can enhance grip strength and barbell control.

4. **Mindful Foot Placement:** The positioning of the feet in the Sumo Deadlift is critical to optimize leverage and force transfer. Lifters should experiment with foot width to find the stance that allows for a vertical shin angle and an efficient hip hinge.

The Conventional Deadlift: Narrow Stance, Total Body Engagement

In contrast, the Conventional Deadlift is characterized by a narrower foot stance, with feet positioned closer together and toes pointing forward. This stance requires a more pronounced forward lean during the lift, engaging the posterior chain and placing greater emphasis on the lower back and hamstrings.

Training Strategies for the Conventional Deadlift

1. **Posterior Chain Development:** The Conventional Deadlift heavily relies on the posterior chain, including the erector spinae, glutes, and hamstrings. Training strategies should prioritize exercises that target these muscle groups, such as Romanian deadlifts, glute bridges, and hamstring curls.

2. **Back Strength and Stability:** With a greater forward lean and more demand on the lower back, lifters should focus on developing back strength and stability. Incorporating exercises such as bent-over rows and back extensions can contribute to a resilient and powerful back.

3. **Grip and Forearm Strength:** While the Conventional Deadlift typically requires a narrower grip, it places significant stress on the grip and forearms. Utilizing grip-specific exercises, such as static holds and pinch grips, can enhance grip strength and support the lift.

4. **Hip Hinge Proficiency:** The Conventional Deadlift necessitates a proficient hip hinge to maintain proper form and engage the posterior

chain optimally. Practicing hip hinge mechanics through exercises like kettlebell swings can reinforce this movement pattern.

Considerations for Choosing Between Sumo and Conventional Deadlifts

When deciding between the Sumo Deadlift and Conventional Deadlift, several key factors should be taken into account:

1. **Body Proportions:** Individual biomechanics and body proportions can influence lifters' preferences and biomechanical efficiency in each deadlift variation. Longer arms and shorter torsos may favor the Conventional Deadlift, while individuals with greater hip mobility may gravitate towards the Sumo Deadlift.

2. **Training Goals:** Training goals play a significant role in selecting the appropriate deadlift variation. If the primary focus is on developing leg strength and targeting the quadriceps, the Sumo Deadlift may be preferred. On the other hand, lifters seeking to engage the posterior chain and build back strength may lean towards the Conventional Deadlift.

3. **Injury History:** Previous injuries and vulnerabilities should also be considered. The Sumo Deadlift places less stress on the lower back, making it a potentially safer option for those with lower back issues. Conversely, lifters with hip or groin concerns may find the Conventional Deadlift more suitable.

4. **Personal Preference:** Lastly, personal preference and comfort in each lift should not be underestimated. Some lifters may simply feel more comfortable and confident in one variation over the other, contributing to better overall performance.

The choice between the Sumo Deadlift and Conventional Deadlift hinges on a combination of individual biomechanics, training goals, injury history, and personal preference. Each lift offers unique training benefits and muscle recruitment

Progressive overload stands as a cornerstone in the journey of mastering the Sumo Deadlift, allowing lifters to continually push their limits and unlock new levels of strength. It is time to delve into the significance of progressive overload in Sumo Deadlift training and provide programming tips to optimize performance and drive consistent progress in this challenging lift.

The Role of Progressive Overload: Strength through Adaptation

Progressive overload is the fundamental principle that underpins strength training, including the Sumo Deadlift. It refers to the systematic increase of training stress over time, driving the body to adapt and become stronger. In the context of the Sumo Deadlift, progressive overload challenges the musculoskeletal system, the nervous system, and the body's energy systems, promoting hypertrophy, neuromuscular adaptations, and improved force production.

Applying Progressive Overload to the Sumo Deadlift

1. **Gradual Weight Increase:** The most apparent aspect of progressive overload in the Sumo Deadlift is the gradual increase in weight lifted. Lifters should aim to incrementally add weight to the barbell in a controlled and consistent manner. As the body adapts to the increased load, it responds by building strength and muscle mass.

2. **Volume Manipulation:** Volume manipulation involves adjusting the total number of repetitions and sets performed during Sumo Deadlift training. Initially, lifters may focus on higher volume training to establish a foundation and reinforce proper technique. As strength improves, transitioning to lower volume, higher intensity training can stimulate further adaptations.

3. **Frequency Management:** Progressive overload can also be achieved through managing training frequency. While beginners may benefit from more frequent Sumo Deadlift sessions to reinforce technique, advanced lifters may find greater benefits in less frequent, higher intensity sessions to allow for sufficient recovery.

4. **Variation and Progression:** Incorporating variations of the Sumo Deadlift and progressing in difficulty over time contribute to progressive overload. Variations such as deficit Sumo Deadlifts, block pulls, or paused lifts challenge the body in new ways, eliciting continuous progress.

5. **Rest and Recovery:** Adequate rest and recovery are essential components of progressive overload. Sufficient rest between training sessions allows the body to recuperate and adapt to the imposed stress, promoting optimal strength gains.

Programming Tips for Sumo Deadlift Training

1. **Warm-Up and Mobility:** Prioritize warm-up exercises and mobility work to prepare the body for the demands of Sumo Deadlifting. Dynamic stretches, hip openers, and activation drills can enhance performance and reduce the risk of injury.

2. **Technique Refinement:** Focus on perfecting Sumo Deadlift technique before emphasizing heavy loads. Incorporate lighter weights and higher repetition sets to reinforce proper form and build neuromuscular connections.

3. **Periodization:** Implement periodization into your training program to promote systematic progress and prevent plateaus. Structuring training into distinct phases, such as preparatory, strength-building, and peaking phases, can optimize performance.

4. **Accessory Exercises:** Complement Sumo Deadlift training with accessory exercises that target weak points and support overall strength development. Accessory exercises may include hip thrusts, Romanian deadlifts, and glute bridges.

5. **Rest Days and Active Recovery:** Allow for sufficient rest days and incorporate active recovery

techniques, such as walking, light swimming, or yoga, to aid in recovery and reduce fatigue.

6. **Progressive Loading:** Gradually increase the weight lifted during Sumo Deadlift sessions. Utilize rep ranges that align with your training goals, such as 4-6 repetitions for strength development or 8-12 repetitions for hypertrophy.

7. **Deload Weeks:** Incorporate deload weeks into your training program to promote recovery and prevent overtraining. Deload weeks involve reducing training volume and intensity, allowing the body to recuperate fully.

8. **Tracking and Journaling:** Maintain a training log to track progress and make informed adjustments to your programming. Recording sets, reps, and weights lifted provides valuable insights into strength gains and areas for improvement.

Listen to Your Body: The Art of Auto-Regulation

While progressive overload is crucial for Sumo Deadlift training, it is essential to recognize the significance of auto-regulation. Listening to your body and adjusting training based on daily readiness and fatigue is critical to prevent burnout and injury.

On some days, the body may not be primed for heavy lifting, and it may be beneficial to focus on lighter, technique-focused sessions or rest altogether. Recognize the difference between soreness from hard training and pain from potential injury, and make informed decisions regarding your training intensity accordingly.

It is essential to balance progressive overload with auto-regulation, listening to the body's signals and adjusting training intensity accordingly. By embracing these training strategies and programming tips, lifters can unlock the art of the Sumo Deadlift, mastering this powerful lift and attaining new heights of strength and performance.

CHAPTER 6: ADVANCED TECHNIQUES AND VARIATIONS

The Sumo Deadlift, a testament to strength and power, has long been revered in the world of strength training. As lifters seek to elevate their performance and explore advanced techniques and variations, the Sumo Deadlift High Pull (SDHP) emerges as a dynamic and explosive option. Let's learn the intricacies of the Sumo Deadlift High Pull, exploring its mechanics, benefits, and application in training, as lifters unlock the art of this challenging lift.

The Sumo Deadlift High Pull: A Fusion of Power and Speed

The Sumo Deadlift High Pull is a versatile movement that combines elements of the Sumo Deadlift and the High Pull, drawing from Olympic weightlifting and functional fitness disciplines. As a hybrid movement, it demands precise coordination, explosive power, and a strong foundation in Sumo Deadlift technique.

Mechanics of the Sumo Deadlift High Pull

1. **Stance and Grip:** To initiate the Sumo Deadlift High Pull, lifters assume the wide Sumo Deadlift stance, with feet positioned outside shoulder-width and toes pointed outward. The grip should be wide, hands gripping the barbell just inside the knees.

2. **First Pull:** The first pull of the Sumo Deadlift High Pull mimics the initial phase of the Sumo Deadlift. With a neutral spine and engaged core, lifters drive through the legs, extending the hips and knees simultaneously to lift the barbell off the ground.

3. **Second Pull:** As the barbell passes the knees, lifters transition into the second pull, employing explosive hip and leg extension. The hips propel forward and upward, and the heels rise slightly off the ground as the lifter generates power through the lower body.

4. **High Pull:** The high pull phase involves forcefully pulling the barbell upwards with an explosive shrug and pulling motion of the arms. The elbows lead the barbell, pulling it towards the upper chest and collarbone.

5. **Triple Extension:** At the top of the movement, lifters achieve triple extension - extension of the hips, knees, and ankles - creating maximum force transfer to the barbell.

6. **Receiving Position:** After reaching the peak of the high pull, lifters quickly transition into the

receiving position. The barbell should be close to the body, and the elbows should be high, creating a shelf for the bar to rest on.

7. **Return to the Ground:** To complete the movement, lifters reverse the motion, lowering the barbell back to the ground with control and maintaining proper alignment.

Benefits of the Sumo Deadlift High Pull

1. **Power Development:** The Sumo Deadlift High Pull is a potent exercise for developing power and explosiveness. The combination of triple extension and the pulling motion of the arms requires rapid force production, making it an effective movement for athletic performance enhancement.

2. **Muscle Recruitment:** The Sumo Deadlift High Pull engages a wide range of muscle groups, including the hips, glutes, hamstrings, back, shoulders, and arms. This full-body engagement contributes to muscle development and improved functional strength.

3. **Cardiovascular Endurance:** Due to its dynamic nature and rapid succession of repetitions, the Sumo Deadlift High Pull can elevate heart rate and serve as a conditioning tool, enhancing cardiovascular endurance.

4. **Sports Performance:** The explosiveness and full-body engagement of the Sumo Deadlift High Pull make it a valuable exercise for athletes across various sports, such as weightlifting, functional fitness, and sports requiring power and speed.

5. **Variation and Interest:** Incorporating the Sumo Deadlift High Pull into training adds variation and novelty to workouts, breaking monotony and keeping training engaging and challenging.

Programming and Training Considerations

1. **Technique Mastery:** Before incorporating the Sumo Deadlift High Pull into training, lifters should first establish a solid foundation in both the Sumo Deadlift and the High Pull. Proper technique and coordination are crucial to perform the movement safely and effectively.

2. **Light Loads and Higher Repetitions:** As with any advanced movement, it is advisable to start with lighter loads and higher repetitions to familiarize oneself with the mechanics and explosive nature of the Sumo Deadlift High Pull. This approach allows lifters to reinforce proper form and reduce the risk of injury.

3. **Gradual Weight Progression:** As lifters become more proficient in the movement, they can gradually increase the weight lifted to challenge their power output and strength capabilities.

4. **Warm-Up and Mobility:** Prioritize a comprehensive warm-up and mobility routine before attempting the Sumo Deadlift High Pull. Focus on dynamic stretches and activation drills to prepare the body for the demands of the movement.

5. **Appropriate Footwear:** Proper footwear, such as weightlifting shoes or minimalist footwear, can provide stability and support during the Sumo Deadlift High Pull, enhancing performance and reducing the risk of injury.
6. **Integration into Training Program:** The Sumo Deadlift High Pull can be integrated into training programs that emphasize power development, strength, and sports-specific performance. It can serve as a dynamic accessory exercise or as part of a complex training routine.

7. **Listen to Your Body:** As with any advanced movement, it is crucial to listen to your body and avoid overtraining. Rest and recovery are vital components of optimizing performance and preventing injury.

Incorporating this dynamic movement into training programs offers a host of benefits, including power development, muscle recruitment, and cardiovascular endurance. When programmed and executed correctly, the Sumo Deadlift High Pull serves as an effective tool for enhancing sports performance and overall strength development.

The Romanian Sumo Deadlift emerges as an advanced technique that warrants attention. Endeavor to learn the mechanics, benefits, and programming considerations of the Romanian Sumo Deadlift, as lifters strive to master the art of this unique and challenging variation.

The Romanian Sumo Deadlift: A Fusion of Strength and Control

The Romanian Sumo Deadlift, also known as the

Romanian Sumo Deadlift High Pull (RSDHP), blends elements of the traditional Romanian Deadlift (RDL) and the explosive Sumo Deadlift High Pull (SDHP). As a hybrid movement, it demands not only strength but also exceptional control and mastery of movement mechanics.

Mechanics of the Romanian Sumo Deadlift

1. **Stance and Grip:** Lifters assume the wide Sumo Deadlift stance, with feet positioned outside shoulder-width and toes angled outward. The grip should be wide, hands gripping the barbell just inside the knees.

2. **Hip Hinge and Lowering:** The Romanian Sumo Deadlift begins with a controlled hip hinge, pushing the hips backward while maintaining a neutral spine and engaged core. The barbell is lowered along the thighs, with the lifter maintaining a slight bend in the knees throughout the movement.

3. **Stretch Reflex:** Unlike the traditional Romanian Deadlift, where the barbell is lowered to the floor, the Romanian Sumo Deadlift utilizes the stretch reflex to reverse the movement. The barbell is lowered only to just below knee level, allowing the hamstrings to stretch while retaining tension.

4. **Reverse Movement:** From the stretched position, the lifter forcefully drives the hips forward, extending the hips and knees simultaneously to return to a fully upright position. The barbell is pulled upward, close to the body, using a

combination of hip and arm extension.

5. **Triple Extension and Pulling Motion:** At the top of the movement, lifters achieve triple extension - extending the hips, knees, and ankles - generating maximum power. The arms then initiate a pulling motion, guiding the barbell towards the upper chest or collarbone, similar to the high pull phase of the Sumo Deadlift High Pull.

6. **Receiving Position:** In the receiving position, the elbows are high, creating a shelf for the bar to rest on the upper chest or collarbone.

7. **Controlled Lowering:** To complete the movement, lifters reverse the motion, lowering the barbell back to the starting position with control and maintaining proper alignment.

Benefits of the Romanian Sumo Deadlift

1. **Hamstring and Glute Emphasis:** The Romanian Sumo Deadlift places significant emphasis on the hamstrings and glutes, making it an effective exercise for developing strength and hypertrophy in these muscle groups.

2. **Control and Mobility:** Performing the Romanian Sumo Deadlift with controlled movement patterns enhances overall body control and mobility, particularly in the hip hinge.

3. **Strength Transfer:** The Romanian Sumo Deadlift fosters strength transfer from the hamstrings and glutes to the arms during the pulling motion, supporting power development and improved force production.

4. **Eccentric Strength:** The controlled eccentric portion of the movement, where the lifter lowers the barbell with tension, challenges the muscles' eccentric strength capabilities, contributing to overall strength development.

5. **Posterior Chain Engagement:** The Romanian Sumo Deadlift engages the entire posterior chain, including the hamstrings, glutes, and lower back, promoting balanced strength development in this region.

Programming and Training Considerations

1. **Technique Mastery:** Before incorporating the Romanian Sumo Deadlift into training, lifters should establish proficiency in both the traditional Romanian Deadlift and the Sumo Deadlift High Pull. Sound technique is crucial for executing this advanced movement safely and effectively.

2. **Moderate Loads and Repetitions:** As with any advanced variation, lifters should start with moderate loads and higher repetitions to hone their mechanics and ensure proper muscle engagement. Gradual weight progression can follow as lifters gain confidence and strength.

3. **Warm-Up and Activation:** A comprehensive warm-up and activation routine, focusing on dynamic stretches and muscle activation exercises, is essential to prepare the body for the demands of

the Romanian Sumo Deadlift.

4. **Footwear and Barbell Positioning:** Proper footwear, such as weightlifting shoes or minimalist footwear, can enhance stability and support during the Romanian Sumo Deadlift. Placing the barbell close to the body during the pulling motion optimizes leverage and reduces the risk of strain on the lower back.

5. **Integration into Training Program:** The Romanian Sumo Deadlift can be incorporated into training programs that emphasize hamstring and glute development, as well as full-body strength and power. It can serve as a potent accessory exercise or as part of a complex training routine.

6. **Rest and Recovery:** Given the higher demands of this advanced movement, sufficient rest and recovery are crucial for optimizing performance and preventing overtraining.

The emphasis on the posterior chain, controlled movement patterns, and strength transfer from the hamstrings to the arms contribute to its benefits for strength development and muscle engagement.

However, mastering the art of the Romanian Sumo Deadlift demands a solid foundation in both the traditional Romanian Deadlift and the Sumo Deadlift High Pull. Lifters should approach this advanced variation with caution, focusing on technique mastery, moderate loads, and proper warm-up and activation.

By unlocking the potential of the Romanian Sumo

Deadlift, lifters can elevate their training and embrace the challenge of this dynamic and rewarding lift, propelling them towards new levels of strength and performance.

The Sumo Deadlift with Chains or Bands: Enhancing Dynamic Resistance

The Sumo Deadlift with chains or bands adds an element of dynamic resistance to the traditional lift, amplifying the challenge and fostering strength gains through the entire range of motion. By accommodating resistance, this advanced variation engages the lifter's muscles in a unique and progressive manner, leading to increased force production and power.

Mechanics of the Sumo Deadlift with Chains or Bands

1. **Setup and Stance:** Lifters adopt the wide Sumo Deadlift stance, positioning their feet outside shoulder-width and toes angled outward. The chains or bands are attached to the barbell and the ground or a secure anchor point.

2. **Initial Lift:** As the lifter begins the Sumo Deadlift, the chains or bands rest on the ground, creating minimal resistance at the start of the movement.

3. **Lifting Phase:** As the barbell is lifted off the ground, the chains or bands come into play, progressively increasing resistance as they lift from the floor. This ascending resistance intensifies as the lifter stands upright, demanding greater force production throughout the lift.

4. **Descent and Eccentric Phase:** During the descent phase, the chains or bands act as a counterbalance, gradually lowering the barbell back to the ground. The lifter must maintain control and stability as the resistance lessens throughout the eccentric portion of the movement.

5. **Dynamic Tension:** Throughout the Sumo Deadlift with chains or bands, the lifter experiences dynamic tension due to the changing resistance provided by the chains or bands. This dynamic element challenges the lifter to maintain stability and technique throughout the entire lift.

Benefits of the Sumo Deadlift with Chains or Bands

1. **Strength and Power Development:** The dynamic resistance imposed by chains or bands stimulates enhanced strength and power development. As the resistance increases throughout the lift, the lifter must generate greater force output, leading to improved overall strength.

2. **Explosiveness and Speed:** The ascending resistance demands explosiveness and speed during the lifting phase. This explosiveness translates to other athletic movements, making the Sumo Deadlift with chains or bands a valuable exercise for athletes seeking to improve their performance.

3. **Stabilization and Control:** The dynamic tension created by chains or bands requires enhanced stabilization and control from the lifter. As the resistance changes throughout the lift, the lifter must maintain proper alignment and control to manage the shifting load.

4. **Overcoming Strength Plateaus:** Incorporating chains or bands into Sumo Deadlift training can help lifters overcome strength plateaus. The progressive nature of the resistance challenges the body in new ways, breaking through performance barriers.

5. **Accommodating Resistance:** Chains or bands provide accommodating resistance, meaning that the resistance increases as the lifter reaches full extension. This mimics the natural strength curve of the human body, making the lift biomechanically advantageous.

Programming and Training Considerations

1. **Technique Mastery:** Before attempting the Sumo Deadlift with chains or bands, lifters should have a solid foundation in the traditional Sumo Deadlift. Mastery of technique ensures proper form and minimizes the risk of injury.

2. **Gradual Introduction of Resistance:** Lifters should introduce chains or bands gradually, starting with a light load to familiarize themselves with the dynamic tension. As lifters become accustomed to the resistance, they can progressively increase the load over time.

3. **Warm-Up and Activation:** Prioritize a thorough warm-up and activation routine to prepare the body for the demands of the Sumo Deadlift with chains or bands. Dynamic stretches and muscle activation exercises can enhance performance and

reduce the risk of injury.

4. **Proper Chain or Band Length:** The length and weight of the chains or bands should be appropriate for the lifter's strength level and training goals. Consulting with a coach or experienced lifter can help determine the optimal setup.

5. **Safety Measures:** Safety is paramount when using chains or bands. Ensure that the chains or bands are securely attached to the barbell and anchor point to prevent accidents or equipment failure.

6. **Integration into Training Program:** The Sumo Deadlift with chains or bands can be integrated into training programs that focus on strength and power development. It can serve as a primary lift or as an accessory exercise in a periodized program.

CONCLUSION

"Sumo Unlocked: Mastering the Art of the Sumo Deadlift" is a comprehensive guide that delves deep into the intricacies of the Sumo Deadlift, equipping lifters with the knowledge and tools necessary to excel in this powerful lift. Throughout the book, we have explored various aspects of the Sumo Deadlift, from its foundational techniques to advanced variations, each contributing to a holistic understanding of this dynamic movement.

The journey to mastering the Sumo Deadlift begins with a solid foundation in the lift's fundamentals. Chapters on "The Sumo Deadlift: An Introduction" and "Setting Up for Success" provided essential insights into optimal foot positioning, grip variations, and hip and shoulder alignment. Armed with this knowledge, lifters can lay the groundwork for safe and effective Sumo Deadlift training.

As lifters progress on their path to mastery, advanced techniques and variations present themselves as the next frontier. Chapters on "Advanced Techniques and Variations" explored the Romanian Sumo Deadlift, Sumo

Deadlift High Pull, and the use of chains or bands. These advanced variations offer unique challenges, fostering explosive power, muscle engagement, and dynamic resistance, thereby taking the Sumo Deadlift to new heights.

To truly unlock the art of the Sumo Deadlift, lifters must also understand the role of proper form and technique in executing the lift safely and efficiently. Chapters on "Perfecting Your Form" emphasized the importance of back and core engagement, the role of knees and shins, and breathing techniques to optimize performance and prevent injury.

In the pursuit of mastering the Sumo Deadlift, the significance of progressive overload cannot be understated. The chapter on "Training Strategies" shed light on the principles of progressive overload and its application in Sumo Deadlift training, ensuring continual progress and strength gains.

Throughout the book, lifters learned the importance of listening to their bodies, practicing auto-regulation, and integrating adequate rest and recovery into their training routines. These aspects are crucial to maintaining long-term progress and preventing burnout.

As this book comes to a close, readers are encouraged to embark on their journey of mastering the Sumo Deadlift with confidence and dedication. Whether a novice lifter seeking to perfect technique or an experienced athlete exploring advanced variations, the Sumo Deadlift offers a rewarding and challenging path to strength and performance.

May "Sumo Unlocked: Mastering the Art of the Sumo

Deadlift" serve as a guiding light, illuminating the path towards excellence in this remarkable lift. Embrace the art of the Sumo Deadlift, and may it inspire lifters to push their limits, unlock their potential, and achieve new heights of strength and mastery. The quest for greatness in the Sumo Deadlift is within reach - let us embark on this journey together.

Made in United States
North Haven, CT
27 April 2025